I0086404

UNMASKING FEAR

UNMASKING FEAR

Embracing the Gift We Were Given

Anthony Butto
Founder of Journey Evolution

Published by Anthony Butto, A Journey Evolution Project

Contact me:

mailto:anthony@journeyevolution.com

Copyright © 2018 by Anthony Butto

ISBN-13: 978-0692069073
ISBN-10: 0692069070

PUBLISHER'S NOTE

All rights reserved. Without limiting the rights under copyright reserved above, no part of this publication may be reproduced, stored in or introduced into a retrieval system, or transmitted, in any form, or by any means (electronic, mechanical, photocopying, recording, or otherwise), without the prior written permission of both the copyright owner and the above publisher of this book.

The scanning, uploading, and distribution of this book via the Internet or via any other means without the permission of the publisher is illegal and punishable by law. Please purchase only authorized electronic editions, and do not participate in or encourage electronic piracy of copyrighted materials. Your support of the author's rights is appreciated.

This is a work of opinion, the author cannot take responsibility for any decision or resulting consequence the reader may take on the basis of inspiration or influence from this book. All opinions in this book are honestly expressed and considered helpful and thoughtful by the author. Authorial advice does not replace or free an individual from a burden of responsibility or law.

To mom and dad, thank you for helping me make this project a reality.

I appreciate all that you do.

I love you!

Author's Statement

Hey there. My name's Anthony Butto. I'm the founder of Journey Evolution, a website dedicated to empowering individuals and unlocking their potential. I'm also a Personal Empowerment Coach. That means it is my passion and purpose to coach both men and women toward unlocking their full potential by helping them to look within.

It is only when we take a good hard long look at ourselves that we learn about our own value. In discovering and embracing our self-worth, we establish a relationship with ourselves, and we improve our relationship with others.

In this book we will explore our relationship with one of the barriers that prevents most people from reaching their potential, essentially a form of self-sabotage. In this book we are going to explore fear.

How do I know about this fear? Because I've lived it. We've all lived it.

My own fear affected my relationship with myself and with others for many years. It prevented me from opening up and being vulnerable. I was fearful of people's judgments and criticism. I was also fearful of life's uncertainties, so I avoided taking risks and stepping outside of my comfort zone.

In other words, I allowed fear to live my life for me because I was afraid to unmask it.

Does that resonate with you?

It wasn't until recently that I made a shift from trying to run away from my fear and, instead, fully embraced it. I'm glad I did. The truth is our fear provides us an opportunity for a most precious gift.

Fear is not something that needs to be removed. Fear is not even meant to be removed. Fear is meant to help you. It is meant to challenge you in order for you to grow, not stagnate.

That's why I wrote this book. Not to avoid, destroy, or abolish fear. I wrote this book with the intention to help people embrace the fear they've been afraid to look at. The fear that they have allowed to steer their life in such a way that it has debilitated them from enjoying life the way it was meant to be enjoyed.

As you read, you will notice that I share stories about my experiences. These events took place over the course of 2017. It was the year I decided to start fully embracing my fear by stepping outside my comfort zone and to challenge myself. I did so in order to grow. I did it to become a stronger individual who can serve both himself and others better.

It may seem egocentric to use my own personal experience of fear. However, I've chosen to use myself as an example because it's through my personal journey that I'm able to best understand and describe the experience.

Though you may or may not have experienced similar situations to my own, the fear described in each is real for me. It is because of that that I am confident it will be relatable to your life and your desire to unmask and embrace fear, rather than continuing to run from it.

From this point on and throughout this book, I shall sometimes refer to Fear as an individual. I do so to acknowledge him. To give him a presence that we might look at. A voice that we might listen to and then challenge. A body that, in the end, we might wrap our arms around and embrace.

Many different cultures have personified Fear. You find most ancient civilizations had a god or spirit that could be associated with or as Fear. In some cases, they revered it. Now I'm not saying we need to go quite that far with our depiction and discussions of Fear! However, just like those ancient civilizations it becomes easier to understand and imagine Fear when we personify him. Undoubtedly, we will all personify Fear in different ways according to what we fear. Just like any deity, he is both particular and universal.

In the course of our journey, we may even get to partake in our own little rituals. We may get to summon Fear. We may bring him out of hiding and pose him a question or two of our own. So, let's get going. Fear has a busy schedule. He knows and meets everyone, and it would be impolite to keep him waiting.

Contents

Introduction

The Comfort Zone

When you see or hear the word Fear, what comes to mind?

Maybe it's an unpleasant, unsettled feeling within your gut stirring up emotional anxiety, fright, horror, and even panic. A perceived threat that appears to be uncontrollable or unavoidable.

Fear is always waiting within the shadows, plotting, scheming, hiding behind a mask. In fact, Fear hides behind many masks. Masks like vulnerability, failure, not being enough (for the world and for ourselves), judgment, uncertainty, and even death. He can stir up quite a bit of emotion for those who have allowed him to hold power over them. We will examine each of these masks and how they often comingle across this book.

Before you go on, ask yourself what it is you are afraid of. Have you given Fear permission to keep you stuck in your comfort zone?

Ah yes. The comfort zone. That place where everything stays the same and nothing new or exciting happens. Where familiarity and commonality lead to predictability, boredom, and stagnation. Where we stop growing, where we regress.

Are you stuck in your comfort zone?

Maybe you don't even realize you're stuck. That's the most dangerous trap of all. When you are trapped and don't know it yet. The longer you stay there, the longer Fear quietly and mischievously builds its wall around you. And as time goes on and you grow older, that wall becomes harder to breach.

You may be wondering why you need to do anything at all. Well, visualize a turtle and its shell. What happens when that turtle gets frightened? It pulls back. Into its shell. Its comfort zone. Think about that turtle and the inside of that shell – the turtle all cramped up, dark, lonely, still a bit scared.

Imagine being trapped in that shell all of the time. What if I told you that there is no need to imagine it because all you needed to do was look around. You are already living it, or have at one point in your life. Can you honestly call that living?

You are that turtle, all pulled back into your shell.

You're comfortable yet you're afraid. Afraid to experience what's outside of what you've known and grown accustomed to for the majority of your life. Afraid of Fear who keeps you trapped there. You're afraid to step beyond what you think is safe.

It's time to unmask Fear and lay eyes on him. To challenge him. Embrace him.

Whichever mask Fear wears, you must be brave. You must face him. If you don't, your life will remain exactly as he wants it to be. Are you going to let him win?

What has avoiding Fear cost you? What has it prevented you from experiencing? How long have you allowed Fear to keep you stuck in the same patterns? More importantly, how long will you continue to allow it? Another five years? Ten?

> *"You may not often realize it but stepping outside of your comfort zone is where all of the good stuff happens."*
> *- Anthony Butto*

Are you ready to take that first step beyond the wall Fear has quietly built around you? Are you ready to loosen the grip Fear has had on your life? Are you ready to embrace Fear and start living?

Well, let's do this!

Mask One

The Fear of Vulnerability

"Vulnerability really means to be strong and secure enough within yourself that you are able to walk outside without your armor on. You are able to show up in life as just you. That is genuine strength and courage. Armor may look tough, but all it does is mask insecurity and fear."

– Alaric Hutchinson, Living Peace

Being Seen

People fear being vulnerable with their emotions. Why is this? Well, to be vulnerable is to be exposed. It is to be at risk of being attacked or harmed, either physically or emotionally.

Everyone must fear being vulnerable from time to time. It's only human. We couldn't be vulnerable intentionally with everyone. There's lots of good things out there but also lots of bad things. You should always endeavor to keep yourself safe, and sometimes this desire for safety leads to the fear of vulnerability.

Do you fear being vulnerable with your emotions?

Are you afraid sharing how you feel would make you appear weak or less than the person you want people to believe you are? Are you allowing that fear of being seen to keep you closed off from yourself and others?

What if I told you that being vulnerable allowed you to begin healing any inner pain that you are still carrying from the past? What if being vulnerable left you light and free as opposed to feeling weighed down and drained? What if being open with other people amplified and enhanced your relationships, allowing you to form deeper, more meaningful connections?

All of those things sound great, don't they? Yet, so many of us fear being vulnerable. Not only with others but with ourselves.

We have this false belief that we are weird or broken. Perhaps that whatever pain we have experienced has damaged us, and that to accept ourselves and openly express that acceptance would cause us more harm than good.

We think being vulnerable would cause further hurt. We think we would surrender our personal power to others and lose control of our self-image. By exposing the real us we would be letting down our guard, and that it wouldn't be pretty.

Self-exposure can seem scary. Growing up in a society where the majority of people believe vulnerability to be nothing but a weakness can make self-exposure terrifying.

What happens though when you continue to keep yourself closed off rather than opening up?

Have you ever been stuck in a traffic jam? Take a second now and visualize that. Cars are bumper to bumper. Exhaust is filling the air. Horns are blaring even though there is clearly nowhere to go.

What feelings come to you? Are they feelings of happiness? I would like to bet against that.

That's what it's like when we refuse to acknowledge ourselves and bury our emotions. It's like an emotional traffic jam within you. Everything stays stuck inside you because you are afraid to open up. There is no clear path for movement or progress. That stagnation is something we experience every day.

Imagine that emotional traffic jam within you. Think about how refreshing it would be to clear out your internal highways, no longer hiding yourself from others or trying to mind-read what other people are thinking.

One of the best scenes from the movie *Mean Girls* is where one of the girls says she can predict the weather, granted, as it's happening... but nonetheless she believes she has the power of ESPN or something.

I often joke with people when I'm not sure what they are struggling with. That I don't have ESPN. So it helps to open up a bit and let me know what's going on inside.

Some people get it and appreciate my humor. Others look at me weird and have no idea what I'm talking about. The point is that no one experiences anyone else's experiences. We all understand the world for ourselves and this means we can sometimes struggle to understand others. We are separate, and that makes people feel lonely.

Imagine if we could express what is going on within us perfectly, so that others could instantly know and learn from us. Imagine if others could share themselves with you. With no judgment and with the potential to learn and heal.

Well, it is possible. That's what vulnerability is. It's an honest sharing of ourselves with ourselves and others. Moving beyond the fear of vulnerability unlocks an untapped strength you may never have thought possible.

I know that strength. How? I've experienced it firsthand, by allowing myself to be vulnerable. It wasn't easy for me. You don't just do it once and then it's always possible. To be vulnerable is a choice. You have to judge from moment to moment when to be vulnerable. It can be challenging to do.

Let me tell you a story about myself. Let me tell you about how I opened myself up to vulnerability, how my journey of embracing Fear began. After all, by sharing this I'm being vulnerable. By being vulnerable in this way and in this book, and in front of so many readers, it'll let me grow further. After all, how could I ask my readers to be vulnerable if I can't show them some of my own vulnerability? So, enough of the generalities and the jargon. Let me tell you about my relationship with Fear.

> *"To share your weakness is to make yourself vulnerable; to make yourself vulnerable is to show your strength."*
> *– Criss Jami*

It was a cold winter's night, back on February 2nd, 2017. Why do I remember that date so specifically? Because it was the night before the release of my first book, *Self-Evolution: Break Free and Discover The Real You.* This is not a shameless plug. Although if you haven't read it yet and you are feeling disconnected or de-motivated, feel free to check it out.

You would think the night before your very first book release would be an exciting time, right?

I mean, it is rather empowering to acknowledge that you have a published book in your portfolio.

However, it wasn't very exciting. At least not for me. For me, it was anxiety. Anxiety caused by Fear, who was keeping me company that night.

I had begun writing the book three months prior. It was right around the end of October 2016. All of the Halloween festivities were in full effect and I was in full-blown writing mode.

The funny thing was, up until that point, I was not a writer. I had never written anything beyond classroom book reports and college papers. Yet there I was, pouring my heart and soul into those pages, uncovering things about myself as if I was peeling the layers of an onion.

I was on a mission. A mission of my own self-discovery. In doing so I had to be vulnerable with myself. It was something that I was not accustomed to... at all.

I was never an open person. Being open wasn't something I did. The fear of being vulnerable lamented me with a false belief that sharing my emotions made me appear weak. I felt I would be less of a man for doing so. I kept everything bottled up. (Think back to that traffic jam analogy. My inner highways were backed up for miles and miles.)

You would think as I was writing the book, with a clear intention of people reading it, that my fear of vulnerability would have held me back. That it would have stopped my fingers from vigorously tapping away at my keyboard.

But Fear cleverly hid himself within my determination so as not to rattle or remind me of how open I was being.

Back to that night, the night before the release. Fear was no longer hidden. He was front and center, partying like a rock star while I kept overthinking and questioning what I was about to do and why...

With the official release of this book, I was about to open myself up to not only my family and friends but the world. It felt like I was about to cartwheel out onto a stage, naked. If you haven't guessed, cartwheeling onstage while being naked is pretty vulnerable. Lots of stuff happening there!

Think about it, what would be worse for you? Exposing your naked body to friends, family, and a mass number of strangers or exposing your emotions, insecurities, challenges, and flaws to that same audience?

Actually, in that moment, I probably would have preferred cartwheeling naked.

Sleep was not my friend that night. It was long and restless. However, the big day finally arrived (or I should say morning). Around 8am was when I officially launched what would be the start of my journey of evolution and embracing Fear.

Now, I say "officially" because the book was already live on Amazon the day before. You might be saying, "Wait a second, you've been sharing this story building up to the release and the book was already available?"

Yes, the book was live, but here's the thing. It was like trying to find a needle in a haystack. No one knew about it or where to find it... Until now. With the book link all queued to go, I was about to give my launch group of over ninety people the precise location of where to find it.

Still sleepy-eyed from the lack of sleep the night before, I was shaking as I finished typing up the Facebook post. My mouse hovered over the post button, and Fear sat beside me doing everything he could to distract me.

He rambled nonsense like:

Are you sure you want to do this?

Do you really want to tell people about your insecurities and struggles?

Think of how weak this is going to make you appear.

Fear was making one last attempt to prevent me from pulling the trigger. He wanted me kept in my comfort zone. A cage of his making. And yes. I was scared. Yes. I was nervous. It went against everything I believed as true about vulnerability, that it led to weakness. I knew, however, that if I didn't follow through, Fear would remain in control.

That wasn't how I wanted to live any more.

For me, the whole experience of writing the book felt like giving birth. Not that I know anything about childbirth! I just mean it was life changing, and that it was draining.

With that said, the release of the book felt like the separation anxiety a parent experiences when they send their child off to college for the first time. Nervousness. Worry. Helplessness. Having absolutely no control over it whatsoever.

I hit 'publish post'. There was no turning back. At that moment, those feelings I just described melted away. Fear had gotten up and left the room. He was still in my house, but he was no longer sitting on my lap.

Over the next several days, my emotions ran on edge. The reviews started coming in. To my surprise, people were embracing my first born with open arms. They were connecting with the challenges and struggles I had shared with them. The book had helped them begin to look within themselves where they hadn't attempted to before.

I remember this empowered feeling come over me. I was proud of myself. Proud of being able to break through that fear and step outside my comfort zone. It wasn't weakness I was experiencing in that moment. It was strength. It was the strength to step out from behind the mask that so many of us wear, to help others see that they are not alone in their struggles. It was the strength to stand up and be free. Between the amount of tears I shed, and how long they had been due, I had experienced an inner cleansing.

> *"One of the most important things you can do on this earth is to let people know they are not alone."*
> *– Shannon L. Alder*

Most people view being vulnerable as appearing weak, so they hide themselves. If they allow their true selves to be witnessed it would be like exposing photo film to sunlight. It would ruin their perceived self-image, their relationships with others. They think that they are the only ones who have struggles and challenges and won't be accepted or loved if they express what is going on inside.

That is so far from the truth. Being vulnerable is a way to form deeper connections and to help heal any inner turmoil and pain. It makes you human. Makes you real.

We are raised in a society that often views emotions as weak, especially coming from a masculine perspective. I am hoping that we can break that bias, because the fact of the matter is we are all human and we all experience the same struggle.

To embrace Fear is to be vulnerable. It is to share, laugh, cry, support, and guide each other through the trials and tribulations of life that we all struggle with at one point. Vulnerability, not hiding behind a mask, is what helps us grow.

Trust me, I know about that mask. I hid behind it for a long time. Now I embrace the strength my vulnerability provides. Fear no longer has a dominating hold on me. Don't get me wrong. Fear likes to visit every now and again, but I don't allow him to linger.

Here are a few points to help you unmask and embrace that fear of vulnerability:

- Understand and realize, you are not weird. You are human. Just like everyone else. We all experience the same feelings and emotions. You are not alone. Even though our struggles and challenges are unique to our experience, the emotions we feel are the same. To hide those emotions from the world is to deny our connection with each other.

- Being open will make you more of a person, not less. When others see you being vulnerable, it often provides the space and comfort for them to do the same. It opens the opportunity to bond with people beyond the surface-level conversation most people typically engage in.

- Let go of other people's reactions and opinions. Not everyone will agree or resonate with you. That's ok. It's not about trying to please anyone, it's about being true to yourself. Being true to yourself removes the heavy weight we carry while masking who we are from our fear of being vulnerable.

Avoid these common mistakes:

- It is not necessary to start running through the streets with a megaphone shouting all of your issues in order to break through your fear of being vulnerable. It's not about having to share everything with everyone all the time. Vulnerability is the ability to open up when you feel it can help others and being ok with yourself to do so.

- Realize that just because you are now choosing to be more open that not everyone in your circle of family and friends will be at a level ready to hear and accept it. It could be overwhelming, especially if you have years of built up clutter. Like dipping your toe in a cold pool, start slow.

Start with someone closest to you. Go at a pace that is comfortable for you and the people you are sharing with.

- Don't beat yourself up if people's reactions are not always positive. Their reactions are based on their own thoughts, beliefs, and life experiences. Remember your why. Remember you are choosing to face Fear for your personal growth to become a stronger person.

If you fear being vulnerable, if you are refusing to open up, imagine wearing a backpack. This backpack doesn't come off. It's with you when you are awake and when you are asleep. It's attached when you are out with friends and when you are home alone.

As time goes on, that backpack gets heavier and heavier. Why is that?

In that backpack is all of the internal crap and emotional pain you continue to carry around with you. Fear of vulnerability keeps you from opening it up and cleaning it out.

> *"What happens when people open their hearts?"*
> *"They get better."*
> — *Haruki Murakami, Norwegian Wood*

Time to unmask this fear.

Take some time to examine what you've kept packed up and buried deep down inside of yourself. Write out the things that you've been afraid to share. Things that if you did share you would feel lighter, relaxed and free.

Look at that list. How heavy is your backpack right now? The physical act of writing alone can begin to help alleviate what you may have packed away. You may not have even realized what has been buried within you for so long.

As you look at your list, is there anything that you can begin to share with the people closest in your life? In the next few days could you open up and move forward? Allow a deeper connection to grow within yourself and those you love.

Take action now.

Mask Two

The Fear of Failure

> *"It is almost impossible to not triumph to bigger and better things, if you aren't afraid to make mistakes, learn from them, and try again with a better approach."*
>
> *– Edmond Mbiaka*

The Challenge

So we come to the second of the masks that Fear wears. The fear of failure.

It is a mask everyone will recognize. There is something in everyone's life that they have failed at. Failure is a part and parcel of life. If we did not fail we could not succeed. Every action we might take is loaded with both the possibilities of success and failure. More importantly, no failure is absolute, and likewise as we will come to learn in this chapter, no success is either. There is no perfection, though in order to take on any endeavor we reach toward it.

Sometimes we can carry our perceived failures for a long time. I say perceived because commonly our failures are not as severe as we might believe. They can do us harm like this. They can make us scared to try new things. Whether physical, emotional or mental, failure can weigh so much. In certain contexts, failure is a terrifying mask to behold.

So let's begin by asking what new things you are afraid of trying because you're not sure how they will turn out. Do you constantly strive for perfection, trying to avoid making mistakes at all costs? Quite simply, are you afraid to fail?

What if I told you that by letting go of that fear to fail you will open yourself up to new opportunities, life lessons, and greater successes than you would have been able to experience had you continued to shy away from that fear?

Ask yourself how often you allow the fear of failing to dictate your actions, avoiding anything different because, let's face it, from a certain perspective there is zero threat of failing at something if you never try.

Why do we allow this to happen?

Well, we are taught at a very young age that failure isn't favorable. We spend the majority of our childhood and young adult lives in a system where we are constantly evaluated, graded, and compared to our peers.

Consider school. Receiving an A grade represented the best, and, may in turn have inflated the ego. Contrast this to receiving an F, which often discourages us, deflating our self-worth and fueling our fear of failure. Yet, when it comes to the real world, all those grades don't necessarily mean you will succeed at what you strive for. Those grades could leave you with a negative self-perception or a false sense that everything moving forward will be easy. Neither one fully prepares you for the trials and tribulations of life.

I've received plenty of high grades and honors throughout my academic career. I can honestly say none of them have helped define my character more than the lessons I've learned about myself through my failures.

However, when we are young we don't comprehend the benefits of failing. What is it about failure specifically, beyond our learned belief that it is bad, that holds us back? That keeps us stuck in our comfort zone?

Perfection. The need to be perfect.

Even though total perfection does not exist, sometimes we feel that in order to succeed our actions have to be "perfect" from the start at everything we do. With no room for error and without that level of certainty, we avoid taking any action at all.

Without a doubt, Fear is a killer of dreams.

Imagine if every child was born with the fear to fail. If that were the case, then even walking and talking would be non-existent. Children would be too afraid to try. It is the reverse which is true. Children tend to be the most curious and happy. They ask questions. They wander about. They have not yet experienced loss or pain to such a degree that they fear the world around them. They have yet to meet Fear. Perhaps we can infer from this that the fear of failure is just a belief that was learned as we grew up. Failing isn't bad. We were just taught that it was. And as we live with it, and we experience losses and difficulties in our lives, that belief, that fear of failure, grows stronger as we move in to adulthood.

This culminates in many adults being afraid to take risks and try anything new. They continue to live life afraid. Afraid to pursue their dreams and passions. Does this resonate with you? Has the fear of failure ever stopped you from trying or pursuing your passions? If so, is holding on to that fear worth the cost of doing nothing?

I know all about this mask. For me it has been one of Fear's favorites to wear. I allowed my fear of failure and my perfectionistic ways to hold me back for many years. Even now, it can still get the best of me. However, it's through failure that we learn to improve, adapt, and grow. In order to extinguish that fear of failure you have to be willing to fail.

> *"There is only one thing that makes a dream impossible to achieve: the fear of failure."*
> *– Paulo Coelho, The Alchemist*

It was Wednesday, March 22, around 9pm eastern time. I had recently returned from dinner with a friend (vegan food – surprisingly tasty) when I decided I would jump on Facebook to do a quick live video.

I had allowed Fear to crank up the intensity of my anxiety when it came to doing live video. The prospect of taking pictures had always made me camera shy. The prospect of live video wasn't any better.

I did manage to step outside my comfort zone to do a couple of videos prior to that, but I was quick to return. Fear still hung tight with me, although he had become a pinch less hyperactive compared to my first video attempt (which I remember well).

I remember doing that first video like it was yesterday. There I was, sitting on my bedroom floor, getting ready to do my first Facebook live video attempt.

Fear was sitting on the couch behind me. I could feel the heaviness of his presence. My breath was shallow. Gazing at the "Start Live Video" button staring back at me, Fear whispered into my ear, "Go ahead push it." He knew full well I didn't want to.

I write the word "attempt" specifically because the very first video I recorded never actually made it. Oh, it was live for those few minutes, but I somehow accidentally deleted it afterwards. I am pretty tech savvy so don't ask me how I could have done that. I think it was Fear's childish way of getting back at me for trying to shake his grasp.

Back to that night of March 22nd, I took a couple of deep breaths and started the video. As people started slowly tuning in, I began discussing probably one of the greatest topics of all time. The commonality between snails and turtles (besides having a shell). Can you guess what that is?

Patience.

Well, it was more about pointing out the importance of practicing patience within our own lives that I was discussing, but I'm sure you got the gist.

You might be thinking, "Anthony, that's great. What does the topic of that night's video have anything to do with this story?" Absolutely nothing. I just thought it would be cool to mention it in case you were curious and wanted to go check it out. (@EducateEngageEvolve. All of my original videos are still out there. Yikes.)

Where was I? Oh right.

Back to the story, one of things that had been on my mind prior to doing that video was how I could better connect with people in a more meaningful way. Yeah. I had done a random video here and there but I was looking for something more consistent. Before ending that video, I openly called out myself to commit to a 30-day challenge where I would do a live video every night for the month.

I mentioned earlier that Fear had been losing his hyperactivity. I had been slowly breaching his wall. However, in that moment when I made the commitment, it was as if Fear just swallowed a bottle of caffeine pills and washed them down with energy drinks.

Do you have a dog?

You know when they are lying in the corner, just chilling out or maybe a little bored because no one is paying much interest to them, and then all of a sudden they hear a noise, a car door or something... Their ears immediately stand up. They jump around. They start running all over the place.

That was Fear... And he knew I was ready to start playing his game again.

I was freaking out. What was I thinking? I had a hard enough time getting through the few videos I had already managed to do, talking about snails, turtles, and patience. What the heck was I going to talk about every day for the next thirty days?

Would I be able to do this? What if I mess up? This is going to be a complete disaster...

Fear was loving it.

The next evening arrived. With my self-declared challenge in effect, it felt like my virginity to live video had miraculously been restored. The nervousness and anticipation were building. I tried to maintain my composure but my heart felt like it was running a sprint when it had only prepared for a leisurely jog. The pressure had been so small before, but now...

I didn't want to let anyone down. I didn't want to let myself down. I didn't want to fail.

In the beginning, every night was a hurdle. With each video, I often stumbled over my words or rambled on and on aimlessly. With each video, Fear eagerly awaited and expected me to quit. He was ready to point his finger, laugh his ass off.

And yeah... it wasn't perfect. There were a number of times I questioned whether or not I was providing value. It was like when a handful of construction workers stand around a big open pit in the highway, all watching the one guy in there actually doing the work. At times, I felt like I was one of those bystanders.

Most nights, I didn't know even what the heck I was going to talk about. If I did plan something out, it usually changed minutes before it went live! (Anthony's secret formula for success - just go with it and hope for the best. Use at your own discretion.)

Here's the thing.

With every day that passed I grew a little stronger, less afraid. It didn't matter if I tripped because I kept moving forward. I didn't allow anything to throw me off course. I made a commitment to others and to myself to follow through no matter what.

Although I would not say I'm a pro by any means, by the end of the thirty days, I realized that without ever taking that first step you will never really know who you truly are and what you are capable of achieving. To embrace Fear is to step beyond your comfort zone with a willingness to fail. It's the ability to fall down seven times and get up eight. It's to know that without failure there is no growth. Instead, failures allow you to become a stronger person.

> *"The one who falls and gets up is stronger than the one who never tried. Do not fear failure but rather fear not trying."*
> *- Roy T. Bennett, The Light in the Heart*

Most people view failing as a bad thing. They are afraid to risk the mistakes needed to succeed. They would prefer a life of regret because they are unable to recognize that it's through the process of failing that the doors to greater opportunities open.

Failing is a necessary part of life. I believe to fear failure is to give yourself permission to remain stuck, never branching out beyond what you know. When you allow the fear of failing to hold you hostage in your comfort zone, you don't allow yourself to try new things. Things that you may discover you love, or could learn to love.

With every failure you get one step closer to success. So let's take a look at a few ways of unmasking Fear. After all, it's not only important we know what to look for when dealing with Fear, but also how to act, unmask, and embrace him.

Here's how to get started with unmasking your fear of failure:

- Challenge your belief that failure is useless. Question if that is actually true. Realize that even the most successful people failed at one time or another. It is impossible to grow without trying and impossible to try if you are afraid to fail.

- View mistakes as nothing more than the stepping stones needed to help you learn and improve your performance. Even Superman had to crash and burn a few times before it was up, up, and away.

- Tap in to that brave inner child that tried everything with no hesitancy. As a child, the word failure was not even in our vocabulary. From walking, talking, to riding a bike, we didn't think twice about it. The trips and stumbles along the way didn't stop us from moving forward. So why should it now?

Avoid these common mistakes:

- Thinking there is always a right way and a wrong way of doing something. Yes, there are basic principles or general guidelines involved to accomplishing something. However, even the greatest athletes and musicians achieve things in ways that best suit them. The only wrong way is doing nothing at all.

- Quitting after your first attempt. Thomas Edison had to fail thousands of times before creating the light bulb. He was quoted as saying, "I have not failed. I have just found 9,999 ways that do not work." Michael Jordan didn't quit when he missed a shot or lost a game. He notes, "I've missed more than 9000 shots in my career. I've lost almost 300 games. 26 times, I've been trusted to take the game winning shot and missed. I've failed over and over and over again in my life. And that is why I succeed."

• Believing you can't, even before starting. You have to let go of the belief that you can't. If you start out with the belief that you can't then you won't. You will never know until you try so just get started. It's better to say you tried than to say I wish I gave it a shot.

If you are currently struggling with that fear of failure take a minute and think about how it's held you back in your life. Think about how you've avoided taking risks or trying new things because you were afraid of what the outcome would be.

Think about what you've given up on. What hopes, dreams, interests, or passions have you let fall to the wayside? Whether a new skill, hobby, starting a business, pursuing your passions, or experiencing a relationship, you can only get better through repetition. If you are afraid to make that first attempt you will be forever limiting your life experience.

> *"If you don't try at anything, you can't fail... it takes back bone to lead the life you want."*
> *– Richard Yates, Revolutionary Road*

The unmasking continues.

What has your fear of failure kept you from trying or doing? Start making a list of all of those things you have always wanted to start but have been afraid to. Maybe it's the business you've always wanted to start but never did. Or maybe it's that instrument you've always wanted to take up but didn't because if you couldn't just pick it up and play with ease you felt it would be impossible to succeed. Remember, repetition is the mother of skill.

We all have wants and dreams that have fallen by the wayside. Things that when we look back on we are plagued with a question of, "What if...?" Things that Fear and his mask of failure have terrified us into abandoning. Well ask those what ifs now and write them out. See them in front of you. Embrace them.

Then, once you've made that list, go back and pick your top three. The ones that really stand out. The ones that you need to try in your life. Of those top three, which one is the most meaningful to you? Determine what you can do within the next twenty-four hours to step outside of comfort zone and take that first step.

Mask Three

The Fear of Not Being Enough

> *"As long as you look for someone else to validate who you are by seeking their approval, you are setting yourself up for disaster. You have to be whole and complete in yourself. No one can give you that. You have to know who you are - what others say is irrelevant."*
>
> *– Nic Sheff*

Who Do You Think You Are?

The fear of not being enough. One of Fear's more intricate masks. Intricate because it usually involves other people at a certain stage through comparison and contrast, and because, like the other masks Fear wears, it is one painted in hues of uncertainty.

We could start with a definition of being enough; *adequate for the want or need; sufficient for the purpose or to satisfy desire.*

But a definition is only going to go part of the way. To unmask this one we are going to have to go deeper. We are going to have to ask ourselves questions such as:

Do you fear you are not enough?

Have you ever tried to be something you are not in order to prove your worth?

Are you constantly beating yourself up, thinking that somehow you should be more, do more, be a better child, parent, worker, spouse, friend, and, that in your own mind you don't measure up?

If you've answered yes to any or all of those questions, you are not alone. The fear of not being enough is a potent fear every human being will experience at one point. People react to this mask in different ways. Some overcompensate, some undercompensate. We don't want to do this. What we do want to do is, just like always, we want to unmask Fear and embrace him. We need to understand this mask first.

So what does it really mean to fear not being enough?

Many people try to strive to satisfy other peoples' expectations and opinions. Generally, we're prone to trying to compare ourselves with others. We try to emulate similar styles, characteristics, reactions that we deem are worthy of love and connection. We do so to attract that same love and connection. This leads us down a road where we copy and mimic others without really considering what we are doing, what it really does for us and others. This image of perceived worthiness will vary based on everyone's unique experience.

Love and connection are perennial human needs. We instinctively pursue these needs to feel complete and happy. It's no wonder then that people compare themselves with others or try find common ground, even if it's superficial ground. Ironically, the need for love, combined with our fear of not being enough, can lead us the wrong way.

Why do we allow this to happen?

Like most of the fears discussed in this book, it's because of learned conditioning.

Think about this. We are born in to this world free of judgment, thought, and fear. As newborns we are accepted and loved just for being alive, just for being us.

Then, as life unfolds, as we begin to absorb and learn, we become a bi-product of our surroundings. We become an effect of something else. All of that incoming information is stored in our brains, establishing roots that grow stronger and stronger over time. It is these roots that set up the thoughts, patterns, and beliefs carried with us our entire lives.

Sometimes those influences are not healthy for us. Whether they be family, school, society, peers, neighborhood, they can be dangerous. Not that they certainly are, just that they can sometimes be. It takes experience and a little wisdom to identify this. The key to knowing is if these influencers begin to manifest a sense of lacking within ourselves - the fear that we are not enough.

Can you think back to a moment, maybe even several, where someone told you that you were not good enough at something?

If so, did you automatically believe it? If you are reading this right now, I'm going to assume the answer is yes.

How did it make you feel? Was it empowering? Probably not.

As we continue to grow up, we carry around this fear of not being enough in our adult lives, focusing on what we don't have versus what we do. We fear that who we are as a human being isn't good enough, constantly comparing ourselves to those around us instead of just being who we are. In time we disconnect from ourselves. We stop acting like ourselves in our desperate attempt to be someone else. It is important to remember though, that no one can be anyone else completely. Even in our attempt to be someone other than ourselves, we are still us, under the mask.

On top of all that, we are bombarded with products that marketing and advertising imply would complete us. They take the inner journey and try to replace it with the outer. These products are insubstantial. They will never make a meaningful difference.

But, you must agree, the advertisers do an amazing job, don't they? Having us believe that without these things we will never find love, never be successful, never be accepted.

However, no one can determine what makes someone "enough." Enough of what? Can you really define what makes you "enough"?

I say the answer to that is no. No, because there is no legitimate answer. It's complete bullshit. It's unattainable. There is no such thing. You are already enough by the sheer fact that you are alive. We let this fear control us in such a way that we feel a sense of lacking, an emptiness.

I can say from my own experience that this particular mask of Fear's never left me feeling good about myself. Even now, Fear still kicks my ass more often than I'd like. Those roots run deep... However, here's what I learned...

> *"You are already whole. Be the person you want to be. Don't be someone else in order to please someone else."*
> *– Anthony Butto*

As I glanced over at the clock on my office wall, I realized I only had thirty minutes left. Thirty minutes left to prepare what I was going to say. Thirty minutes left to figure out how I would be able to prove my worth. Because, in thirty minutes, I was going to experience my first interview...

I remember one afternoon, a few weeks prior, I had been scrolling through my email. I was checking to see if there was anything of actual importance other than the nonstop spam mail I typically receive (can you relate?), and I came across an invitation to be a guest on the *Fear Not* podcast. Founded and hosted by Billy Atwell, Billy interviews individuals, neuroscientists, and other mindset specialists each week to inspire people to live a life beyond their fears.

It had only been a month or so since embarking on my new journey and purpose, starting with my book launch. I was now being asked to interview on a show which had previously included top medical doctors, professors, authors, and coaches.

My excitement was powerful enough to blanket Fear and accept the invitation. However, Fear eventually squirmed out.

I was afraid I was not enough.

Less than thirty minutes before my interview and there I was, this kid from Medford, Long Island, about to be interviewed on a show entitled *Fear Not* to discuss how to overcome Fear. I was scared out of my mind. Oh, the irony... And there was Fear, lounging in the corner, staring at me with a big grin on his face.

As I continued shuffling through my notes, trying to collect my thoughts, I reluctantly looked over at the clock above me again. Ten minutes left. It was as if everything went dead silent. Except for the clock.

I could feel the sweat under my arms. This is going to date me but, it was like I was wearing one of those shirts that changed color based on your body temperature. Could you imagine what my shirt would have looked like had I been wearing one?

Clearly, my antiperspirant was not working.

Then I hear the phone. It was like the alarm you would hear back in school when there was a fire drill. Show time. As I pick up the phone, Fear gets up from lounging, rushes over, and leans next to me as if eavesdropping on our conversation. I was trying to calm my nerves. Billy and I conversed a little bit before commencing the interview. The good thing about the interview was the fact that it wasn't live. Knowing that did lower my anxiety slightly, but once I heard him say that we were recording, it cranked back up.

Throughout the interview Fear was dancing around me. I tried to stay cool, calm, and collected. The whole time, like a broken record, Fear kept repeating, "Who are you to give advice about facing me or about anything for that matter? Who do you think you are anyway? You are nothing special."

Have any of those thoughts raced through your mind? Whether in a relationship, a professional environment, or in a family setting, have you experienced similar thoughts? What were they? How did it make you feel?

If it was anything like I was feeling back then doing that show, I'm sure it wasn't good.

Oh. Something else to point out. Remember those notes I mentioned I prepared prior to the call? Well about 99 percent of what I wanted to say from those notes never made it. (If you want to know what actually did come out, you can listen to the full interview located on the homepage of my website, journeyevolution.com.)

The interview lasted about forty-five minutes or so. I'd like to say those forty-five minutes flew by but it felt more like a draining forty-five hours. After the interview was over, I let out a big sigh of relief. Still not even knowing what the heck I had just said, the pressure I placed on myself to prove my value had dissipated.

Billy and I continued to have a casual conversation for about an hour or so after that, further sharing our stories and experiences. We've actually become good friends in the process.

One of the most important lessons I learned... was I didn't necessarily need to be a world-renowned expert or doctor or really anything else in that moment other than being me. I was already whole. No one can ever take that away from me unless I let them.

I didn't have to prove anything to anyone. I was living my life based on my purpose, my values, and what I believed in while unmasking Fear in the process. In doing so, I gave people the opportunity to connect with the real me. You could say that by unmasking Fear, I was unmasking myself too.

The value I was providing was based on what I've experienced in my journey which is unique to me. If I was able to help and inspire just one person to embrace their fear than it was completely worth it.

Similar to you, no one will ever be me. See through my eyes. Hear as I hear. Learn, grow, and experience life as I do. Acknowledging that is worth more to me than anyone's definition of being enough.

> *"The most important day is the day you decide you're good enough for you. It's the day you set yourself free."*
>
> *– Brittany Josephina*

Most people believe that they are not enough. They fear they are not good enough, strong enough, smart enough, pretty enough, pretty much a fill-in-the-blank list that goes on and on. They never recognize their worth. They downplay the value that they provide by not acknowledging their strengths and remain focused solely on their weaknesses.

Fear traps them in an imaginary pursuit as they try to fill all of these missing pieces they believe are lacking within them. Rather than encourage growth in a healthy, supportive way, it fuels the dysfunctional cycle of scarcity.

We are who we are. We should not try to live up to someone else's expectation of who we should be. It's time we stand up to Fear. We should not allow him to continue to have an impact on how we define ourselves.

You can't enjoy life if you are trapped in the fear of constantly lacking something, feeling the need to be someone or something other than you. You are you. No one can ever take that away without you giving them permission to do so.

There are lots of reasons why expectations fall on us, even if they come from seemingly innocent origins. Everyone will have felt the weight of expectation at one point or another. It's one of the masks Fear wears. In order for us to see it clearly, we must know how.

Just like before, let's go through some steps to unmasking Fear:

- Question who or what is it that you think you are not enough for. Question why you feel that way. Everyone will have their own opinion and perception of you and that doesn't mean it is you. Once you recognize what that false definition is that you are trying to live up to, you can begin to loosen the grip it has on you.

- Love yourself. Appreciate yourself. We often forget to acknowledge our strengths and solely focus on our weaknesses. This has us feeling less than. However, both our strengths and weaknesses make us who we are. Take advantage of your strengths (a.k.a. super powers) and improve upon your weaknesses.

- Focus on living your life in accordance with what you want. Never live in the way other people want or expect you to be. You will never be able to live up to everyone's expectations nor should you have to. We were not born to please others but to share with them our own gifts and uniqueness.

Avoid these mistakes:

- Thinking you no longer need to do anything to improve yourself or your life. On the contrary, instead of trying to improve for others, which comes from a place of lack, you are now doing it for yourself. Grow for you.

- Showing feelings of anger, resentment, or bitterness toward those who made you feel like you weren't enough. Take time to forgive and let go. People don't often realize the unrealistic expectations they place on others. Love, compassion, and empathy are still possible while staying true to yourself.

- Don't be an asshole. Being able to embrace your value and self-worth does not devalue anyone else in the process. Respect yourself and show respect for others. We are all living on this big blue orb together.

We've all experienced the fear of not being enough at some point or another. It's ok. You are now aware of it. That said... will you allow the fear of not being enough to limit who you are or who you want to be?

What has it cost you so far? How much of yourself have you sacrificed trying to fit into someone else's definition of who they want you to be as opposed to just being you? How much are you willing to give up in order to meet everyone else's needs?

It's time to let go.

Like any of the other masks Fear wears you will see this particular mask more than once in life, even when you feel you've already dealt with it. Fear has regularly approached me while wearing this mask, the mask of not being enough. Don't try to be someone or something else. Be the person you want to be for you and you will begin attracting abundance in to your life.

> *"Maybe my best isn't as good as someone else's, but for a lot of people, my best is enough. Most importantly, for me it's enough."*
>
> *– Lindsey Stirling, The Only Pirate at the Party*

It's time to unmask Fear.

To work on this fear, it's important to determine what triggers it. That means asking questions about the expectations we and others put on our life.

We have to ask why we feel like there are these expectations in the first place. Firstly, society is a place in which people are constantly comparing one person to another. Between school, work and family life, people are prone to making generalizations and establishing standards to regulate image and behavior. Some of these standards are good. Standards like law, standards like health and safety. However, we have a tendency to go further and restrict harmless or honest behavior. It's easy to see how you could go too far and create expectations which are destructive by being narrow.

Another origin of expectation could be living up to the standard someone else sets. Sometimes by comparing ourselves with someone who is seemingly better at something than us, even if it's for innocent purposes, we can feel inadequate. We begin to ask why we aren't at that level yet. It can hurt. Such an expectation can do more damage than good, especially if the person we admire or like makes demands on us that we can't fulfill. Sometimes these people have their own issues they're bringing forth, sometimes it's less intentional on their part. It leaves us feeling inadequate, trapped, even if there are things we can do that they can't.

Start making a list of those instances when you feared you were not enough. Look deeply into your own life, at all the people who demanded something of you, even when it wasn't fair to do so. Write out the standard you believed you needed to live up to in order to feel worthy. Then, list out who or what determined that standard and why you think it hit you so hard. What were the consequences of these standards?

Once you can begin to see where it originated and what it is about, you can begin to recognize and accept that it does not define who you are. You get to choose the person you want to be. No one else.

Mask Four

The Fear of Judgment

> *"Criticism is just someone else's opinion. Even people who are experts in their fields are sometimes wrong. It is up to you to choose whether to believe some of it, none of it, or all of it. What you think is what counts."*
>
> *– Rodolfo Costa, Advice My Parents Gave Me: and Other Lessons I Learned from My Mistakes*

Stop Staring At Me

J udgment. Yet another of Fear's masks. Specifically, the judgment others have of us.

It's unavoidable. We judge all the time in order to understand and qualify our world. From understanding what's good to eat to buying a car, judgment gives us the means to prioritize better ways of being. When it comes to people, people are always judging each other and themselves. Of course, judgment is closely related to the previous mask because to judge can lead to expectations and standards. If the judgment is bad, perhaps the expectation or standard is too.

So when does Fear approach us wearing his mask of judgment? Well, there can be many situations in which judgment may be feared or avoided. Often these are situations when the opinions of others can hurt us or injure our self-worth. Take for example speaking in front of a group of people. Most would be able to speak in front of friends. Not many would speak so honestly in front of an audience.

Public speaking is in fact considered the top fear in America, followed by the fear of death (which I will talk about later in another chapter). When it comes to public speaking, it's not necessarily the actual physical action of speaking in public that has people freeze up like deer in headlights, is it?

No. It goes deeper than that. It's the underlying fear. A fear which is typically triggered by the act of having to speak in public.

It's the fear of judgment.

Does that resonate with you? Because Fear and his mask of judgment is the focus of this chapter.

Everyone everywhere will be judged by another person sometime, somewhere, at some point in their lives. Whether that means being silently judged or having it spoken aloud, it will happen, multiple times and on multiple occasions. People are always judging. They can judge something good, they can judge something bad. Judgments can change over time or judgments can, like people, stagnate.

With this being true, why then do we fear it? If judgment is going to happen and we know it is, why do we allow this fear to keep us stuck in our comfort zone?

It comes down to having a deeper understanding of our judgment and where it stems from.

Our judgments can be reflections of our own insecurities. To quote Carl Jung, "Everything that irritates us about others can lead us to an understanding of ourselves." When we fear being judged by others, what we assume is that they are judging us based on how we view ourselves. If you took two people and asked them what they were afraid of being judged on, their responses might be similar in nature but would be specific to their self-perception.

The judgment we fear is based on what we think are our flaws. We live trying to hide what we perceive as negative or unacceptable about ourselves to the outside world.

The last thing we want is for someone to pull back the curtain and shed light on all of the crap we falsely believe about ourselves.

But here's the thing. Those judgments made about you by other people have nothing to do with you at all. Those judgments are based on the insecurities of the people doing the judging.

As I mentioned before, our judgments are a reflection of our own insecurities.

So, if that wasn't confusing enough, let me go ahead and reiterate that we fear being judged based on the negative beliefs we hold about ourselves, however the judgment by others is based on their own internal landscape. Judgment is a mirror.

So, by allowing the fear of judgment to keep us stuck, we hide ourselves, and when we hide ourselves, we can't be who we really are. In essence, we are valuing other peoples' opinions and beliefs ahead of our own.

Who are you? Are you able to be yourself without any concern or worry about what someone else might think or say? And if so, how has that played a role in the way you've lived your life up until now?

Fear has shown up quite often for me over the years in his attempts to prevent me simply being me. I tried to portray a persona in order to hide my insecurities, not realizing that any judgment from others was actually based on how I felt about myself.

However, what I've learned from my unmasking of this Fear is that...

> *"When you continually worry about what other people think of you, they own you."*
> *– Donald L. Hicks, Look into the stillness*

It was right around Easter. A rainy evening in April. I was on my way to my first Meetup group for public speaking.

I pulled up to what looked like an old abandoned house. It was similar to one of those creepy houses you might see in a horror movie. I questioned whether I was in the right place, and after double-checking the address, sure enough, this was it.

I got out of the car. As I turned to make sure the doors were locked, there he was. Fear was sulking in the passenger's seat, pressed against the window. But, I could've sworn Fear's frown turned upside down at the very last second, as if he knew something I didn't and I was about to find out.

I stepped into the old house from the rain. The floor boards creaked. I thought to myself, "This was an odd place for a meeting to practice public speaking but, hey, what do I know?" It was the typical horror movie scenario playing out right in front of my eyes; I was the hapless stranger walking straight into the killer's trap.

I continued to walk down the hall toward a sign that said 'Toastmasters'. Before I could peek in to the room to check out what was going on, out jumps a guy wearing a white bucket hat like the one Gilligan wore in the show Gilligan's Island (for those young enough not familiar with the show, feel free to Google it so you can get a sense of what I am referring to).

I was like, "Is this the public speaking meetup?"

He said, "Yes, welcome to Toastmasters, please sign in, come on in, have a seat."

When I originally signed up for the event a couple weeks prior, there was no mention of it being a Toastmasters meeting, not that I even knew what that was at that point in time anyway. For those not familiar with Toastmasters, the main objective is to give every member an opportunity to practice their speaking skills each week in front of a group.

To do this, each member is assigned to perform various duties. Some of these include Speaker, Evaluator, Table Topics Participant, "Ah" Counter, Grammarian, Joke Master, Table Topics Master, Timer, to name a few.

This was much more elaborate and way more structured than my expected scenario of sitting around a table at Starbucks talking to a few new people I've just met. Furthermore, according to the meeting invite, there were only four people, including myself, listed as going.

Being an introvert, and mainly dictated by my fear of judgment, this was definitely outside my comfort zone. However, since there was such a small number of people scheduled to attend, I figured this was a fairly safe starting point to begin unmasking Fear.

Now don't get me wrong. I was still a bit fearful of the situation but Fear didn't have complete control over me. Had there been a larger group I clearly would have turtled up, avoided the situation all together and thought to leave. Fear knew that as well.

Jump back to that moment with Gilligan...

As I walked in to the room, the three guys I expected to be there were nowhere to be seen. However, there were about thirty-five to forty other faces I was not expecting to see. Now I understood exactly why Fear had been grinning earlier. I was freaking out.

I took a seat, pretending that the anxiety I was experiencing was enthusiasm for wanting to be there, and Fear took a seat beside me. Unassumingly, I looked around the room, almost as if looking for escape routes. Too late. The meeting was already underway.

Typically, each Toastmasters meeting is divided into three major parts. Prepared Speeches, Table Topics, and Formal Evaluations.

Since I was a newbie and it was my first meeting with the group, I managed to sit there quietly observing, avoiding any real attention, in my unassuming bright pink and blue-checkered shirt. (I'm sure I stuck out like a sore thumb. It's like seeing a clown standing in the middle of the road armed with red balloons. You can't miss it.)

Well, anyway, I managed to sit in silence up until... Table Topics...

Table Topics is considered one of the most challenging elements of communication because it is speaking on the fly. It offers the ongoing challenge to speak in front of a group without preparation. Individual members are called to the front of the room to discuss a subject for a timed two minutes, a subject provided by the Table Topics Master for the day.

Remember in school when the teacher looked around the room to call on someone for the answer and you just looked down at your desk thinking, "Please don't pick me. Please don't pick me." In that moment, that was me... although it didn't work. I was picked. Damn you bright pink and blue checkered shirt...

Now I could have easily said no, I didn't want to participate. But wasn't that the whole point of why I was there? You can't embrace Fear by avoiding him.

So, I got up, and Fear got up with me.

I walked up to the front of the room, having yet to turn around and face the crowd. On the table in front of me was an Easter basket filled with those little plastic eggs you put candy in. The ones used for Easter egg hunts.

Instead of candy, the eggs held the various topics that were up for discussion that night. After shuffling around in the basket and grabbing an egg, I cracked it open and my Table Topic question was, "Are you a morning person or a night person and why?"

Still having yet to turn around and face the crowd, I thought to myself, "I got this" or at least I thought I did.

I took a deep breath and as I did a 180-degree turn, I saw the sea of eyes now staring upon me. Fear skipped around me, saying, "What ya gonna say? What ya gonna say? Go ahead. What ya gonna say?"

The times keeper started the clock and it began.

Just like the podcast interview I shared with you in an earlier chapter, I can't remember what I even said while standing up there.

All I remember was the brightness of the lights, the sweat on my forehead, and an older gentleman in the back-left corner of the room, dressed in a suit, glaring at me as if we were in the championship match of a starting contest. I remember mentioning I was a morning person, going to the gym, and I believe I also made a reference about pizza.

It definitely qualified as one of those on-stage-naked moments I referenced back in Chapter One, but, in this instance, throw in the flavor of a top hat and some jazz hands for flair.

After finishing up whatever it was I rambled on about, I received some applause and took a seat. I did it. No matter what I actually said or what I believed anyone thought of me, I did it.

I came to find out afterwards, I didn't even speak the full two minutes. I only managed to hit the forty-second mark.

Once the meeting ended, I talked to a few of the members afterward and what I learned was that not only was everyone else just as nervous and scared to be up there as I was, no one even remotely mentioned any of my own perceived insecurities I assumed they would have easily spotted.

What I also learned from that experience was that no matter what anyone thought of me in that moment, no matter what judgments there may have been, it was none of my business. And when I left I didn't have to take on and carry any of that with me. Remember, you can never stop people from judging you. You can however stop paying attention to their judgments and move on. You don't have to house anyone else's thoughts in your mind but your own. That is something you get to choose, no one else.

It's an empowering feeling.

> *"A person that judges others will inevitably judge themselves harshly. It is only when one stops judging others that, that one can truly appreciate the beauty within."*
>
> *– Ando Oomae*

Most people fear public speaking even more than death. They avoid it like the plague, limiting their potential in their ability to talk to others, to make social connections, to advance their career, to gain the confidence to speak up for themselves, and to share, motivate, inspire, or help others. They don't see the true nature of what stops them.

It's not the action of speaking in public that holds people back. It's what's beneath the mask. It's the fear of being judged. If you can unmask Fear, you can embrace him. If you can do it, he will allow you to open up more freely, reap the benefits, and take more risks, including having an easier time speaking publicly.

It takes time to do this, and some people will always have difficulty in speaking publicly. Our fear of others and their judgments is proof of the importance others have for us. If you weren't at least a little concerned with speaking publicly you wouldn't care about anyone but yourself.

Face the fear of judgment by:

- Identifying and embracing your insecurities, as well as acknowledging your strengths. When you are able to accept yourself whole-heartedly, you are less likely to be harmed by other peoples' opinions or judgments of you.

- Understanding that judgment by others is unavoidable. Let people judge you all they want. Remember, it has nothing to do with you. If they are not judging you, they will be judging someone or something else.

- Focusing on self-improvement and not what others are saying. If there are certain aspects of yourself that you are unhappy with, make it a priority to invest in yourself. Work on your personal growth.

Avoid these common mistakes:

- Trying to fight fire with fire. Facing your fear of judgment does not mean judging others in return.

- Taking it personally. Although peoples' opinions and judgments may be directed towards you, realize they are actually not about you.

- Isolation. Once you become more aware of what specifically you are afraid of being judged on, you may want to avoid being around people. The key here is to do the opposite. This is the time to get out and experience more social situations and interactions. You don't face Fear by running away but rather leaning in to him.

If public speaking frightens you, what is it you are really afraid of? Is it judgment from others? Think about how Fear has held you back in other aspects of your life. Also, take some time to recognize how Fear affects your daily interactions with people and your overall sense of self.

Imagine being able to embrace this fear and allowing yourself to be the person you always knew you were meant to be. You cannot truly be yourself if you continuously allow the fear of judgment from others to dictate your life and hold you back from following your heart, pursuing your passions, or achieving your dreams.

You are in charge of your life. You get to choose how you want to live it.

"Judgement of others and ourselves always comes from a place of fear. It is fear that keeps us from living authentically all that we say we value."

– Shannon L. Alder

Time to take a closer look at this mask. Make a list of all of your perceived insecurities, personality traits, and physical attributes you believe people are judging you on. They can be anything from any point in your life. They can be recent insecurities or ones you've held for a long time. Ask yourself what they are specifically. What do they mean and how is it do they undermine you? By contrast what is it you do value? Do these insecurities threaten that which you truly value?

Delve deeper and ask yourself if any of them are valid. Remember that everyone is a work in progress and no one is perfect. Understanding deficiency is a means to become better at what you do. Ask yourself what can you change, what can you not? Perhaps on a second glance these insecurities are simply reflections of other people and their insecurities? Go through the list. Determine which ones you need to accept fully and which ones you can begin to work on improving.

Mask Five

The Fear of Uncertainty

> *"I wanted a perfect ending. Now I've learned, the hard way, that some poems don't rhyme, and some stories don't have a clear beginning, middle, and end. Life is about not knowing, having to change, taking the moment and making the best of it, without knowing what's going to happen next. Delicious Ambiguity."*
>
> *– Gilda Radner*

Walking On Fire

Look up from your page or your screen. Look out the window. What do you see? A horizon.

There are things beyond that horizon, but from our position we cannot see those things just yet. If we were to walk all the way to that horizon we would never catch it, never meet it. The horizon would always be further on.

Our horizon is the end of our world, but not the end of the world. That means that our horizon exists on other things too. Our horizon is not just the end of our vision but also what lingers around the bend of the road. It is other people, events, experiences. It is a culmination of all those things we still have yet to witness.

What the horizons harbors then, what it represents for us, is uncertainty. It is all the things we could doubt, hesitate over or consider unpredictable. It is that unpredictability that we are going to talk about in this chapter. We've all experienced it. Uncertainty. To live is to be uncertain. To live is to not know the future, the present or the past completely. To live is to not know everything around you and maybe not even yourself. Uncertainty is in all things.

What uncertainties have you noticed in your life? Regardless of uncertainty being everywhere, which uncertainties are more obvious to you? Which uncertainties make you anxious? Do you avoid taking risks because you cannot guarantee you will achieve your desired outcome?

Do you shy away from anything new or different? Are you constantly in need of control in one or more aspects of your life, almost to the point that straying off that rigid path of what you know scares the crap out of you?

If you answered yes to any or all of these questions, pause for a minute or two. Think about how the need for certainty has steered your life, even though uncertainty is everywhere. Think about all of the decisions and actions you've taken or didn't take and how it has led you to this very moment.

Did everything you expected would happen in your life, based on your assumed path of certainty, actually happen?

I mean is anything in life ever truly certain or guaranteed?

That is the funny thing about life. Life itself is the most honest definition of uncertainty. To attempt to control that uncertainty would be to deny yourself life.

Our fear of uncertainty cripples us from wanting to change what we are already commonly familiar with. It often leads us down a road of commonality, boredom, and predictability that steal away the essence of life.

You see the human need for certainty is strong. So strong, in fact, that we are subconsciously willing to watch the same movie, multiple times, even though we know how it ends, because we liked it the first time so we are sure to enjoy it again. To choose another film may not produce the same enjoyment.

We are willing to go to the same restaurants, over and over, eat the same dishes, because we don't necessarily want to risk trying something new and potentially not liking it.

We are willing to stay in the same job for years even though it provides us with no enthusiasm, inspiration, motivation, or sense of fulfillment. We do so because we have no way of knowing for sure whether it would turn out better if we decided to choose a different path.

We are willing to stay in toxic relationships even though they hurt us because at least we are certain of what to expect. We would rather endure the suffering than risk stepping out into the unknown to find that love and connection we desire and never finding it.

Doesn't this sound crazy? Yet, for many, this is "Life." Why do we do this?

We are afraid that things will end up worse than they are, though in some cases it is already pretty bad.

Have you ever seen the movie *Yes Man* where Jim Carrey, playing the role of a risk-averse banker, goes to a life-changing seminar where he agrees to say yes to every opportunity that comes his way, even though his typical reaction would be no?

Have you ever been like that? Passing on life's many opportunities because of the fear of uncertainty? Constantly worrying about a future that has yet to arrive?

Is that what life is supposed to be? Doing the same things day in and day out, in an attempt to maintain a perceived level of safety and security?

For many years, that was my life. I was that risk-averse banker I described earlier. I avoided uncertainty, staying in a job I didn't like with no intention to ever leave because it felt "safe."

Remaining in unhealthy relationships for years and years because even though I may not have been happy, I was familiar with the feeling. I knew what to expect.

It wasn't until I began unmasking that fear of uncertainty, not knowing what is going to happen next and still moving forward, that I became more alive. It was about letting go of trying to control my future and allowing myself to be open to what life was about to show me... Here's what happened...

> *"When you lose your path, you get an opportunity to discover a world you have never known! And better worlds are often found this way! Darkness and uncertainty hide presents in itself!"*
>
> *- Mehmet Murat ildan*

It was after 11pm on a humid Thursday night in the middle of July when I found myself walking barefoot down the streets of Newark, New Jersey... and I wasn't alone. I was surrounded by thousands of others, all marching towards the alluring sound of drums and the warm glow of Tiki torches off in the distance, chanting one word over and over in unison, "YES. YES. YES."

To an outsider looking in from afar, they may have assumed the zombie apocalypse, portrayed on a number of popular television shows so many times, had now finally become a reality.

Imagine, for a second, waking up in the middle of the night to a rumbling sound. You look out your bedroom window, eyes half open, and witness a sea of strangers all moving in one direction as if they were a herd of cattle off to the slaughter. Creepy, right?

As my thousands of newly acquired friends and I moved closer to our desired destination, there were three distinct odors I experienced that night I will never forget... the smell of kerosene from the tiki torches, the hot coals, and feet... lots of feet.

So, you may be asking at this point, what was this all about? What was going on?

This was the first night of my attendance at Tony Robbins' four-day seminar, *Unleashing the Power Within*. Tony is a world-renowned Life and Business Strategist, and on the first night of this event is Tony's famous fire walk.

For those of you who are wondering what a fire walk even is... Well, fire walking is an ancient ritual practiced by different cultures around the world to demonstrate strength, courage, and faith. It is intended to help people conquer their fears by walking across hot coals.

Walking over those hot coals is a symbolic experience that proves if you can make it through the fire, you can make it through anything, and that's what I was about to do. Fear and my uncertainty about what to expect, on the other hand, had other intentions for me though.

The drums were much louder now. The air hotter from the coals. The masses of people slowly thinned out, as each made their way across those coals sprawled out over a long stretch of road. As my turn approached, I began to recall the four guiding principles Tony directed us to do in preparation for this moment:

1. BE IN A PEAK "STATE."

It was important to possess a deep sense of self-assuredness. The energetic and supportive group environment is critical to helping everyone get and stay in their peak "state." Hence, the thousands of barefooted strangers I mentioned earlier, all chanting in unison.

2. WALK, DON'T RUN.

Do not run across the coals. Walk. Running like you are in a race against both Superman and the Flash is bound to lead to injury as running pushes your feet deeper into the embers, which can burn the tops of the feet.

---

[1] www.tonyrobbinsfirewalk.com/what-is-the-tony-robbins-firewalk/

3. CONTROL YOUR INNER VOICE.

Positive experiences don't just happen. You have to make them happen. By focusing on a word such as "YES," it replaces a negative with a positive which can help you get through anything.

4. BELIEVE IN YOURSELF.

To get through the fire, you have to have the unstoppable belief that you can and will succeed. Focus on the task at hand. When you lose focus, fear begins to creep in and that's when you begin to falter.

Think about this. Have you ever seen those karate guys that punch through stacks of bricks? It was kind of like that. They have an absolute belief that they can and will punch through those bricks because who, in any other state of mind, would think it could be done?

Back to that night...

Three more people... That's all that was standing between me and uncertainty. I had no idea what to expect other than that I was about to step into some crazy hot fire.

Oh, I almost forgot another important thing Tony mentioned not to do... Don't look at the coals!

With that being said, I'm assuming you know what happened next, right?

I was doing my best to keep my focus on everything but what was laid out only a few feet in front of me. That's when Fear whispered in my ear, "Look." With all that was going on, I had almost forgot Fear was there walking alongside of me.

As my attention turned toward the hot coals, I witnessed two of the event workers unloading fresh, bright orange, burning coals right on top of the area I was about to cross.

Holy freaking out time, Batman!

I want to give a quick shout out to Fear because in that moment my peak state went right out the window.

I don't even remember seeing the other three people go before me when all of a sudden it was my turn. I calmly tried to get back in peak state but honestly who was I kidding? It was more like a frantic last attempt at scrapping together whatever composure I could get back while Fear was dancing to the Tiki drums.

The first step...

And I took that first step... one I will never forget.

If I had to describe it in one word... Scorching! I'm not even sure if that really describes it. Imagine dipping yourself in cooking oil and laying on the sun... Yeah, that...

For a split second, Fear jumped out in front of me, paralyzing me in my tracks. I say only for a split second because at that moment I felt as if I was injected with a shot of pure adrenaline. I immediately came to my senses. Standing there was not an option. I looked up, stared Fear right in the eyes, and charged forward, pushing him out of the way as if he were a ragdoll.

I'd say it was about seven or eight steps from that initial one but I am not sure. I was so determined and focused on just getting across that I didn't concentrate on anything else.

The next thing I knew was that I was safely on the other side, my feet were being hosed off, and the level of empowerment I felt was incredible. Fear was nothing more than a puppy at that point.

If you are wondering, "Did I get burnt?"

Yes. My right foot got a little toasty on that first step. Fear won and broke my state, but it was only for a slight moment. Once I broke past his wall he couldn't hold me back from that point on.

We often hold ourselves back from experiencing life because of we are afraid of what might happen or we automatically assume something bad will happen as opposed to what we will gain once we face it.

Yes. There were a couple of negative side effects from that experience (a few heat blisters, which lasted a couple of weeks); however, the inner strength and self-confidence I gained from accomplishing it was worth it.

It's about facing Fear. Taking that first step into the unknown. It's forcing yourself to venture out beyond those walls Fear quietly builds up around you to hold you back, to keep you comfortable.

It's impossible to always know what's going to happen or to see everything that is beyond the horizon. However, it's only by embracing uncertainty we get to live. Because we all know life is unpredictable. To live a life focused solely on certainty leads to an unlived life.

> *"With uncertainty, there is never a dull moment."*
>
> *– Haresh Sippy*

Most people fear uncertainty because they are afraid of experiencing anything different than what is familiar. To stick with what they already know is more comfortable. It provides a level of unconscious safety and security, even when it's causing a negative impact in their life.

Most people would rather endure the familiarity of suffering and predictability. To experience anything different is considered risky if it can't be guaranteed.

I believe that by embracing the gift of uncertainty we open ourselves up to new experience, opportunity, and growth. Letting go of the constant need to know the future, releases feelings of worry and anxiety and allows one to step beyond their comfort zone. The horizon will always be there. No matter if you step away or toward it.

Now, I'm not saying that when you wake up tomorrow you need to immediately leave your job, family, and friends to venture off on an African safari to play with lions and ride elephants. Although that would be pretty bad-ass. However, it's my hope that you use this as a wake-up call to examine your life as it is. Add some spice to what I refer to in my previous book, *Self-Evolution*, as living as a zombie. Embrace uncertainty rather than fearing it.

Here are a few ways to help you with Fear and his mask of uncertainty:

- Open yourself to possibility, not outcome. An amazing attribute of water is its ability to be fluid, flexible, and adaptable to its environment. It molds and shapes itself to the situation. When facing uncertainty, this is an opportunity to be like water in a sense.

It's as Martial Arts Expert, Bruce Lee said, "You must be shapeless, formless, like water. When you pour water in a cup, it becomes the cup. When you pour water in a bottle, it becomes the bottle. When you pour water in a teapot, it becomes the teapot. Water can drip and it can crash. Become like water my friend." Being open and flexible to possibility allows you to fully engage with the experience instead of holding on to the rigidness of an expected or unrealistic outcome.

- Preparation. You may not be able to predict your future but you can help alleviate your fear by preparing for it. Taking steps to prepare for a situation will keep you encouraged to continue leaning in to the unknown as opposed to staying tucked in your comfort zone. Learn, read, witness. Draw on the thoughts and experiences of others to help develop your own point of view, but never neglect your own experience.

Common mistakes to avoid:

- Stop overthinking. Prior to making decisions and taking action, many of us try to think things out, playing the scenario in our head to get a sense of how the outcome might turn out. If the result is favorable we move forward, however if we think for a second there is a chance it won't, we pull back like frightened turtles.

- Avoid Massive Change... at least in the beginning. Full immersion in to the fear can be extremely beneficial for some, claiming it's exactly what they needed to overcome their fear. However, for others, it can be overwhelming, almost crippling, to their well-being. If you are someone who has allowed uncertainty to stop you in your life, start out slow.

If you think that by playing life safe you will experience all that life has to offer, think again.

Imagine standing in the middle of a cornfield. As you look around, surrounding you are corn plants as high as fourteen to sixteen feet tall with the exception of one worn down path. You have no idea what extends in those other directions. So you head down the familiar path in front of you, the one you've walked for years and years.

Although you crave something different, you choose that familiar path because it feels safer. You continue to walk down that lonely path that you're familiar with. The path of least resistance. But there is nothing new down there. Nothing ever changes.

Take a minute now to think about all those things you've missed out on because of this fear. Now answer these questions. Is there anything you have given up on because you were too scared of the unknown? Is it worth sacrificing adventure in order to have a false sense of security?

Maybe it's time to embrace a different direction. Today is the opportunity to start creating a new path in that field and see where it leads to.

> *"Go somewhere you know nothing about and see what happens."*
>
> *– Karl Ove Knausgård, Min kamp 5*

It's time to face your fear of uncertainty. It's time to not only embrace uncertainty within your daily routine but also to start taking small steps outside of your comfort zone to create new experiences in your life.

Let's make a list.

We'll begin with two columns. On the left-hand side, list all of the things you routinely do on a daily basis. On the right-hand side, list all of the ways you can do those things differently. It could be changing what you have for breakfast, or taking a different route to work. Get creative.

Also, list out all of those things you've wanted to try but your fear of uncertainty held you from taking action. It could be a dance class, learning a new language, or traveling to a different state to explore the landscape.

You can't predict the future. So stop trying.

After you've taken the time to review that list, pick which ones are most meaningful to you. Write down what steps you're going to take toward them. Take them by the end of the week. I want you to challenge your beliefs. I want you to start taking action. Don't just think about and write your lists down, plan how you're going to follow through and then hold yourself to it.

Mask Six

The Fear of Death

> *"To fear death, gentlemen, is no other than to think oneself wise when one is not, to think one knows what one does not know. No one knows whether death may not be the greatest of all blessings for a man, yet men fear it as if they knew that it is the greatest of evils."*
>
> *– Socrates*

Flying Like Superman

Death is defined as the end of a person or organism's life. The permanent ending of vital processes in a cell or tissue.

I know I did not need to provide this definition to you. I know you are fully aware of death's meaning.

However, you may not be aware that sometimes the fear of death prevents a person from living at all. It is like dying before one's time. Trapped in the fear of death's eventuality that, one day, when you meet death, there may not even be a life to steal from you.

Is the fear of death keeping you nestled in your comfort zone? Does it prevent you from growing as an individual?

No one wants to die. Yet every day we are dying. We are always slowly moving toward it.

It's inevitable.

It's unavoidable.

It's guaranteed.

It's this fear of dying, however, that keeps so many people from doing anything they perceive as threatening or dangerous. This varies based on what each individual is scared of. Ironically, sometimes things we are not aware of are more of a threat to our well-being than the things we think about constantly, and sometimes things we are very aware of may pose no harm at all. In other words, we can be wrong about what we think, we can be wrong about death.

So where does this perceived danger come from? Why do we let it have a stranglehold on us experiencing life beyond our comfort zone?

It comes from us, as a response to the world we live in. It is a primal feeling, arising when we feel threatened. That feeling is there for a reason. It served us well millions of years ago when we had to escape the salivating jaws of hungry, four-legged beasts.

However, as I mentioned when we first set out on this exploration, you can recognize and appreciate my approach to fear as being learned. Based on what I've discussed throughout our time together, would you not agree that the majority of our fear, unless you are still being chased by wild animals trying to make you their next meal, was taught to us by the environment we grew up in?

Fear's masks, the masks of vulnerability, failure, judgment, not being enough, uncertainty, our fear of death were all passed on to us.

Imagine, for a second, being raised in a culture where death is a celebration, a moving on to a higher greatness as opposed to a mourning of physical loss. How would that affect Fear's grip on our concept of death? In our society, the news and the media feed our fear, amplifying it to insane proportions, almost to a point that many people are scared to do anything. They simply live scared.

Turn on the news for fifteen to twenty minutes. What do you hear?

I'm sure you would agree that there is no shortage of fear-based headlines to keep you on edge.

Headlines like these, consumed on a daily basis, are sure to scare the shit out of anyone. Pay attention long enough and what do you think will happen? You won't want to leave your house.

Whatever happened to trusting our own intuition and having faith that everything happens for a reason? That life serves us for our benefit, not with the intention to harm but to help us grow as individuals beyond what we've been told to believe as threats to our life.

I want you to take a moment now to challenge some of the ideas you've been conditioned to believe. Examine all of the things we perceive as dangerous, challenge the validity of those beliefs. Instead, make a rational decision about it.

If you believe something is going to kill you then it's already won.

Think about it. The things we do on a daily basis are likely to kill us faster than any perceived death defying act we would never try but would love to do.

In reality you are actually more likely to die from fireworks (1 in 340,733), a lightning strike (1 in 79,746), drowning (1 in 1,134), a car accident (1 in 84), stroke (1 in 24), or heart disease (1 in 5).[2]

Anything can happen at any time. Think about all of the little things you are afraid of because of some threat you've been told about.

What experiences and opportunities have you missed because of it?

I'm not here to get in to religion or past lives... I am here to say that we do have this life. My question to you is, "What do you want your life to be?"

This was a question I began asking myself. Even though it took me forty plus years to finally start

[2] https://www.thewildlifemuseum.org/exhibits/sharks/odds-of-a-shark-attack/

asking it, it was those forty plus years that were preparing me for my willingness to face that deep fear that had locked me in my comfort zone.

So, you may be asking, "What did I do to start embracing the fear?"

Great question.

> *"I am not worried about dying, what I am worried about is not living"*
>
> *– Saji Ijiyemi, Don't Die Sitting*

Scrunched up in a little puddle jumper of a plane with four other guys feeling like packed sardines, I hear, John, my instructor, say, "We are at seven thousand feet." As he swung open the side door, exposing us to the outside world, cold air rushed in and hit my face. It was Fear's way of reminding me he was there. As my feet were now hanging outside of the plane, I didn't need his reminder...

"Are you ready?"

Before I go any further... Let me take a step back.

It was a Tuesday morning in September in sunny San Diego, California. If you are familiar at all with San Diego weather, it can usually appear cloudy upon waking up but, as the morning progresses, the clouds dissipate and reveal the beautiful blue sky. It was the morning I was going skydiving for the first time.

I had been talking about doing this for about three weeks prior. The day had finally arrived. Up until then, Fear had not really had much of an impact. It was as if Fear himself was waiting for the right moment to strike, like a rattlesnake stalking its prey.

My friend, Joey, who also decided to make the jump with me, and I arrived at our location, Pacific Coast Skydiving, located at Brown field. After checking in for our reservation, we received a stack of disclaimers that needed to be signed before moving forward. That's when Fear decided to make his first appearance. Not in an overwhelming way. Just enough to whisper, "I'm with you buddy."

After reading through most of the paperwork, and I say most of it because once I agreed to relinquish responsibility of my life on page one, I didn't really see a conflict of interest arising by the tenth page.

That was when the realness of it all hit me like a ton of bricks. I was about to jump out of a freakin' plane! Fear absolutely loved it.

It was still a bit cloudy at that point in the morning. While we waited for the clouds to break, it was a perfect time for John, my instructor I mentioned earlier, to get me all geared up. John was a bit taller and looked a bit older than me. Thin, scruffy, and with long straight hair to boot, he definitely resembled an aged rocker from several of the 80's hair bands I listened to back in high school.

He began running through the various safety rules and precautions. You know, things I probably should have been paying extra special attention to. However, I honestly can't remember much of what he said. It was like ordering through a fast food drive-thru. All I heard were random words... hold on tight... breathe... emergency... second chute... legs up...

I looked over at Joey and I could tell he was starting to experience some anxiety. Fear was working us both.

Shortly after gearing up we were cleared to go.

We piled into the plane, the propellers kicked in and off we went. At about 3000 feet, which was about 3 minutes after takeoff, I experienced a scenic flight over the Pacific Ocean. Flying over Imperial Beach, John was pointing out downtown San Diego, Coronado Bridge, and Coronado Island. As the plane turned around, I was able to see a little bit of Mexico.

Surprisingly, my anxiety had eased up a bit... almost as if Fear had missed getting onboard. I mean, don't get me wrong, I certainly didn't feel like I was in my comfy clothes laying on my living room couch but I wasn't freaking out either... well, at least not yet.

There was one lingering concern on my mind. One of the tips mentioned when you gear up is that the harness should fit comfortably and snugly around your body. One of the most common questions they get when it comes to the harness is, "Is this tight enough?"

That's exactly what I was dwelling on the whole ride up because that thing was clearly way too loose for my liking.

So, of course, I turn around to John, because we had a mere couple of minutes before show time, and ask, "Hey, is this thing tight enough? Do you got me?" His response, "No."

Boom.... There he was... Fear and his mischievous smile.

As John started tightening up the harness, he asked me, "Is there anyone you want to say goodbye to?"

This was all being filmed, of course. I had to purchase the Gold package, which included the video, because the experience of jumping out of a plane wasn't going to do it. I needed to be able to watch it over and over again.

And to John's credit, he did add humor to the whole experience, which I can appreciate now.

"We are at seven thousand feet. Are you ready?"

My response at that moment was not very clear or concise. It was more of a caveman grunt and a head nod.

I was sitting at the edge of the plane, seconds away from experiencing what it is like to fly like my favorite superhero, Superman. However, Fear made sure to remind me one last time of two very important things. One, you are about to jump out of a plane to your potential death... and two, you are not Superman...

Next thing I knew we did a front flip out of the plane and began free falling up to a speed of about 120 miles per hour.

And guess what? Fear was too scared to come along.

In that moment, any worries you may have had, whether it's trying to remember if you paid the electric bill that was a month overdue, or the credit card debt you can't seem to get rid of, or going back to that job you hate, or the argument you had with a family member, are gone.

If I had to describe the feeling of that moment in one word, that word would be freeing.

It was one of the most exhilarating feelings I've ever experienced in my life. You are the most present you could be. The past and the future don't have a hold on you. All of your senses are 100 percent activated. The rush of adrenaline flowing through your body. The sound of the wind as you cut through the air. The vast openness of the sky surrounding you. The sensation of weightlessness as you fall freely, effortlessly, as gravity guides you back to solid ground.

After about a minute of freefall the parachute engaged. John and I spent the next four minutes gliding back down to reality, admiring the view all around us, which was something you cannot experience any other way. It was absolutely breathtaking.

Although part of me was sad it was over, another part of me was thankful I survived.

A few moments after, as I was quickly adjusting to being back on the ground, Joey came gliding down with the same look and feeling that I had. It is an experience and a memory Joey and I shared together. One we will never forget.

Yes, the thought of jumping out of a plane at 7,000 feet can be overwhelmingly scary, but take a minute. Think about what the underlying fear in this case would be. For me, it actually wasn't the physical act that was scary. I mean, I love thrill rides so I am used to those kinds of feelings.

What was the true underlying fear? The fear of death. Taking the risk. Knowing that my life could potentially end in that moment. That I would no longer exist in this world. My physical presence eliminated.

I think that is a fear that keeps most people from living life.

However, I've found from my own experience that having faith and believing in a power greater than ourselves helps fight this fear.

Call it whatever you want; The Universe, God. We all have our own beliefs on this subject and that is ok. As I mentioned earlier, I'm by no means about to get religious here. That is not the purpose or my intent.

However, because I have faith in something greater than myself, I didn't think it was going to end for me that day. Not yet. I truly believe I have a long life still ahead of me. I still have so much to accomplish and so many more people I can help.

Making that jump was not about overcoming heights. It was about trusting in something greater than myself. It was also about becoming a stronger person in the process so I can help spread my message and serve others more deeply.

> *"Don't be afraid your life will end; be afraid that it will never begin."*
>
> *- Grace Hansen*

The fear of death has most people avoiding danger and sacrificing adventure in exchange for a safer way of living, keeping them trapped in their comfort zone. They never stop to challenge their beliefs or trust their intuition.

I believe we are all blessed with the most beautiful gift, Life. To live in fear, scared to do anything other than just "exist," is actually hurting you, not helping you. Trust me, I know from experience. I "existed" for many years.

The bottom line is, however blunt this may sound, you are going to die. Death is a part of life. There are no ifs, ands, or buts about that.

Don't get me wrong. I'm not saying to stand up right now, turn around and live a reckless life. The message I am hoping you can take away from this experience is to challenge what you were taught to believe. Trust your intuition. Have faith. Live. Life's purpose is not to harm you but to make you stronger, help you grow, and experience the beauty of what we've been given.

Here are a few points to help you face that fear of inevitable death:

- Accept death is a part of life. A friend in college many years ago summed it up pretty well back then by saying, "You live, you die." I want to elaborate on that by saying, it's what you do while you live that counts. You get to choose.

- Serve others. Start volunteering your time and energy toward serving others in need. When you are helping others, it will get you out of your own head and in to the hearts of the people you help. Although your physical existence will at some point end, your name, your legacy, and the positive impact you've made on the world will not.

- Put things in perspective. In the grand scheme of things, yes, there is always potential for anything to happen at any time (revisit fear of uncertainty). However, that shouldn't stop you from enjoying the activities that interest you.

- Explore Spirituality. Whether you are religious or not, there are many different ways to open yourself up to spirituality. Let this provide an open invitation for you to explore life in a new way. Acknowledge that each of us is on our own journey. We are all here to serve a purpose beyond ourselves.

Avoid these common mistakes:

- Not using common sense or going with your gut instinct. Some things are just not safe to do, like driving on the wrong side of the road, peeing into the wind, or running with scissors (I've tried that). Challenge your belief, but use your practical judgment and innate gut wisdom to make a decision right for you.

- Going extreme. Facing this fear does not mean you have to follow in my footsteps and go sky-diving or climb Mount Everest or even bungee jump into an active volcano (although that could be pretty awesome, with the right precautions, of course). It's about not letting this fear stop you from enjoying your life to the fullest. Not everything is going to kill you.

Are you going to die? Yes. Will it be tomorrow or the next day? I don't know. No one does. You could assume you have little time left and still get years. You may outlive everyone you know. You might assume you have years and meet your end suddenly. Rather than look for so much that we cannot see, it might be best if we focus on now.

Life existed before you. Life will continue to go on without you. It is what you do with your life while you are alive that is most important.

Embrace Fear. Start living your life!

> *"But you decide how you live your life in the meantime. You can hide fear. Or you can live life. - V"*
> *- Gayle Forman, Sisters in Sanity*

Time to unmask Fear.

It doesn't matter how old you are, there will be things in life that you want to do, that you want to experience. It could be a place that you want to go, an action you want to take.

Once you know what you want, write it down. Start making a list of all those experiences or achievements that you hoped to accomplish during your lifetime, a bucket list if you will, but you simply feared doing. As you look at that list, I want you to think about all of those potentially missed opportunities that you only get this one life to experience. I say 'potentially missed' because you have the power to change that. You can still do those things.

This is about embracing life, not fearing death. This is about opening yourself up to new opportunities and experiences and letting go of perceived dangers.

A life unlived is not a life at all.

Conclusion

Your Story

You're lying on the couch. Binge watching the last season of your favorite show. All of a sudden you hear a knock at the door.

You say to yourself, "Who is that? Should I even bother to get up to answer it?"

Normally you wouldn't. It's not like you were expecting company or had any Amazon deliveries scheduled to arrive that day.

But for some strange reason, you start feeling an urgency stirring within you to do so.

You get up to open it, barely being able to pull your attention away from the hypnotic image box you've been staring at the last couple of hours...

You are stunned.

Standing there is your future self. Even though you can't believe it, you invite your future self in. You offer them a beverage and to have a seat.

Before you even have a chance to ask them anything, still working through the shock, they say:

"I want to share a story about life with you. Our life story. However, it's important to tell you that there are two versions."

You stare back at yourself slightly puzzled. You say, "Ok, let's hear it, older me."

Your future self smiles. "Well then, let's begin."

VERSION ONE

As I look back at my life, I am saddened to say with much regret that I am disappointed by all of the things I didn't do. I lost to Fear. Fear kept me stuck in my comfort zone. He prevented me from truly experiencing life.

I passed on so many opportunities to be vulnerable, to open up, and to share myself with others because I was scared to let people in.

I never took action on all of the creative ideas I had because I was afraid to fail.

I allowed my fear of not being enough to rob me of my value and self-worth, never recognizing my uniqueness.

I let other people's opinions of me dictate whom I was and how to live my life, even though it was me who had ultimate control over my own experience.

I didn't take many risks or give myself a chance to experience anything different than what I had known. I couldn't be certain it would be any better than what it was.

I decided it was best to play it safe. I remained stagnate. I lived my days slowly, dying with each passing moment rather than enjoying what life had to offer.

This is my life story.

VERSION TWO

Looking back at my life, I can say with full conviction that I lived a full and satisfying life. I didn't allow Fear to hold me back. I recognized that Fear was the most powerful gift I had. By embracing him, I got to experience growth.

I was able to experience deep, meaningful love and connection by allowing myself to be seen. This openness invited others to be more open with me.

I explored my passions and interests even if it meant failure because I would rather fail trying than not try at all.

I embraced my value and self-worth, acknowledging that there is and will only be one of me. I discovered my purpose and made a greater impact in the world.

I didn't allow people to define me or my experience because I knew their opinions were based on their own beliefs, experience and perception of me rather than my own.

I let go of trying to control and predict every aspect of my life because it's through uncertainty life shows its true intention, which is to work for me, not against me.

I acknowledged the truth that we will all die one day. That I only have one life to live. That I was not going to let it go to waste.

This is my life story.

So... the real question is...

Which version is your version?

Which version has it been up until this point?

Which version do you want it to be?

If your story isn't the one you hoped it would be because Fear has kept you stuck in your comfort zone, realize it's not too late. It's not over yet. There are still plenty of chapters left for you to write. Tomorrow is a blank page.

You always had the choice as to how you defined your relationship with Fear. However, the past is the past, never to return. How you handle Fear from this point on is up to you.

So, what will it be?

You get to decide.

Thank you!

Thank you for taking the time to read my book!

I hope this book has helped you as it has for me.

I would appreciate your feedback and would love to hear what you thought about this book.

Please leave a helpful review on amazon so we can make a bigger impact for more men and women who need this book.

Please check out my website:

JourneyEvolution.com

You can also email me at:

Anthony@JourneyEvolution.com

Remember, you are not alone on this journey. Together we can become stronger individuals.

Educate. Engage. Evolve.

Thank you,

Anthony Butto

Founder of JourneyEvolution.com

www.ingramcontent.com/pod-product-compliance
Lightning Source LLC
Chambersburg PA
CBHW031537040426
42445CB00010B/575